THE VICTORIA AND ALBERT COLOUR BOOKS

FIRST PUBLISHED IN GREAT BRITAIN BY
WEBB & BOWER (PUBLISHERS) LIMITED
9 COLLETON CRESCENT, EXETER, DEVON EX2 4BY
AND MICHAEL JOSEPH LIMITED, 27 WRIGHTS LANE, LONDON W8 5TZ
IN ASSOCIATION WITH THE VICTORIA AND ALBERT MUSEUM, LONDON

COPYRIGHT © WEBB & BOWER (PUBLISHERS) LIMITED,
THE TRUSTEES OF THE VICTORIA AND ALBERT MUSEUM.
CARROLL, DEMPSEY & THIRKELL LIMITED 1986

BOOK, COVER AND SLIP CASE DESIGN BY CARROLL, DEMPSEY & THIRKELL LIMITED

BRITISH LIBRARY CATALOGUING IN PUBLICATION DATA

SAUNDERS, GILL
TILE PAINTINGS - (THE VICTORIA AND ALBERT COLOUR BOOKS)
1. TILE CRAFT 2. DECORATION AND ORNAMENT
I. TITLE II. SERIES
738.6 NK4670

ISBN 0-86350-147-8

PRODUCTION BY FACER PUBLISHING
COLOUR REPRODUCTION BY PENINSULAR REPRO SERVICE, EXETER
TYPESET IN GREAT BRITAIN BY OPTIC

PRINTED AND BOUND IN HONG KONG BY
MANDARIN OFFSET INTERNATIONAL LIMITED

THE VICTORIA AND ALBERT COLOUR BOOKS

TILE
PAINTINGS

INTRODUCTION BY
GILL SAUNDERS

WEBB & BOWER
MICHAEL JOSEPH
MCMLXXXVII

STRICTLY speaking the illustrations here are not designs for tiles but sketches and tracings of tiles *in situ* or of tiles in the collections of the Victoria and Albert and other museums. The tiles themselves were justly admired, and copies were made as an archive of study material allowing comparison of designs from a variety of sources.

The history and dating of Iznik tiles and the related wares is a complex matter and the subject of some debate. Ceramic production began at Iznik (the ancient city of Nicaea) in the fifteenth century. The so-called 'Miletus' wares once attributed to a town in south-west Turkey have now been established as the earliest products of Iznik. A new industry was established around 1490 probably to supply a growing market in the new Ottoman capital Istanbul, 50 miles to the north-east. In the early phases of production at Iznik, tiles were produced in relatively small quantities and precedence was given to other wares. Demand for tiles suddenly increased around 1550 when the mosque of Suleyman I, one of the great series of mosques, was built in Istanbul. Most of these new buildings were embellished with tile-revetments (walls faced with tiles).

The practice of incorporating ceramics in architectural schemes was established in the near east long before the emergence of Islam in the seventh century: the Byzantine churches for example were remarkable for their mosaics on walls and ceilings. The use of mosaic was absorbed into the

Islamic decorative vocabulary, and in the period preceding Ottoman rule, the thirteenth century Seljuk architecture employed glazed brick – brown, turquoise, purple or blue – as wall decoration. But this technique had only limited pattern-making potential; a more flexible modification was the tile mosaic where monochrome tiles, baked and glazed, were laboriously cut into shaped pieces and then fitted together jigsaw-fashion to create a calligraphic or geometric design.

Attempts to produce polychrome tiles were advanced by the invention of the *cuerda seca* technique (introduced by the 'Masters of Tabriz', immigrant artists from neighbouring Persia): by drawing a line of grease around each pattern-shape several colours could be fired together on one tile without danger of one colour bleeding into another. Tiles using this technique are first seen on the mosque (c.1419-24) and tomb (c.1421) of Mehmet I in Bursa. These are also the first two Ottoman buildings to show a large-scale use of ceramic. The earliest polychrome underglaze tiles were mostly hexagonal with self-contained designs. Towards the middle of the sixteenth century these went out of fashion, to be replaced by larger repeat-patterns floated over a panel of adjoining square or rectangular tiles. (The size of tiles seems never to have been standardized, with new specifications for every building.)

The majority of the designs illustrated here belong to the classic phase of Iznik production, from c.1550 to c.1620. Tiles from this period are characterized by a distinctive colour scheme, including a strong 'sealing-wax' red, so-called because it was thickly applied and stands up from the surface of the tile in perceptible relief. The subtle shades of blue, turquoise, olive green and purple, which identify products of the preceding phase, were replaced by two shades of blue, a true red and a bright copper green. This colour scheme, with the addition of a dominant black outline, appeared for the first time on the *kible* wall (that facing Mecca) in the mosque of Suleyman I (1550-7). Tiles were used rather sparingly in this interior; the mosque of Rustem Pasha (Suleyman's Grand Vizir), completed in 1561, is more lavishly decorated, with tiles used not only on the walls but also on the pillars, in the *mihrāb* (a niche in the wall facing Mecca) and on the *mimbar* (pulpit).

The decorations on these later sixteenth century tiles can be divided into three categories, though it is not unusual to find elements from each used in combination. The earliest of these styles is the *rumî* or arabesque; characteristic *rumî* motifs are foliate arabesques, consisting typically of a split-leaf form, some-times embellished with cusps *(plate 19)* or tendrils. The origins of this motif are complex: the term *rumî* translates literally as 'Romaic' and refers to the Greek lands under Muslim control (initially the Seljuk sultanate in central Anatolia, and later extended to the Balkans). Certainly these arabesque forms can be traced back to thirteenth century Seljuk Anatolia where they appear on tile-mosaic borders in the Medrese of Celaleddin Karatay in Konya. In fact, like so many Iznik motifs, its antecedents may be Chinese, for almost identical border patterns are found in Chinese art of the fifth century AD.

From a simple border motif the *rumî* arabesque was elaborated into a complex all-over pattern which was used on metalwork as well as ceramics. It may in fact have been taken into the ceramicists' *œuvre* via early fifteenth century ceramic copies of metalwork objects. This device can be seen in *plate 20* and again in a more formalized version as a linked chain interlaced with motifs from the *hatayî* style *(plate 2)*. Whatever its origins, the *rumî* motif had a wide cur-rency in the decorative arts of the Islamic world – it appears for instance on the famous Ardabil carpet (No.272-1893 in the Victoria and Albert Museum) from Persia, dated 1539-40.

The *hatayî* style predominated after 1560. The name means 'Chinese' but the constituent elements are often very different from their Chinese proto-types. Rather they are chinoiserie motifs of the 'international Timurid' style. This court-based style, which adapted motifs from the arts of Ming China, was created in the artistic *ateliers* of the capital cities of western and central Asia, including Tabriz in Persia. This was a particularly influential centre in relation to the Ottoman arts – not only were artists and craftsmen imported from Tabriz, but in the long Ottoman campaigns against the Safavids (1514-56) many Persian paintings were looted. Inevitably the decorative vocabu-lary prevailing in Tabriz was absorbed into the work of the Ottoman artists. The *hatayî* style incorporates the *'saz* leaf and rosette' style: these two elements are its most characteristic features. *Saz* is the Turkish word meaning 'reed' – this may be a reference either to the species of leaf or to the reed pen used for the black-ink album drawings which exemplify this style. Typically the *saz* leaf was long, feathery and sinuous. It appears on textiles and in the borders of painted miniatures, as well as on tiles, usually in association with rosettes which offer a formal static contrast to the exuberant curves of the semi-naturalistic leaves *(plates 9 and 23)*.

The third essential element in this style is the palmette, a fantastic flower based on the lotus flower and lotus leaf in combination. This element is interpreted with great variety and invention (compare, for instance, *plates 9, 11 and 22)*. Ultimately it became a composite floral motif incorporating *prunus* blossoms and stylized rose-buds *(plates 2 and 12)*. There are native sources for such composite flowers but their earliest documented appearance is in the early fifteenth century Venetian textiles which circulated the near east.

An indisputably Chinese motif often used in *hatayî* designs is the cloud band. This has a long history in Ottoman ornament, first as small rounded puffs very similar to the original Chinese form, later drawn out into long trailing bands. These are used on tiles to add linear rhythms to predominantly floral designs *(plates 14 and 20)* or formalized into elaborate abstract shapes far removed from the original Chinese motif.

Just how far the appearance of Chinese motifs on, Iznik ceramics was attributable to the potters' familiarity with Chinese porcelain is a matter for some doubt and speculation. Very little Chinese porcelain seems to have reached Turkey before the second quarter of the sixteenth century. It seems more likely that the chinoiserie motifs which appear in Iznik designs were diffused through the arts of other near-eastern civilizations, notably Persia. Here the Chinese influence was particularly pronounced because around AD1300 Mongol dynasties were ruling in China and in Persia with consequently close cultural links.

The Ottoman artist was adept at assimilating details from a wide variety of sources and transforming them to create a synthesis that was distinctively Turkish. Both the *rumî* and *hatayî* styles are evidence of this, but the third style which features on the classic Iznik tiles, the so-called *quatre fleurs* style, was an indigenous Ottoman development. It is named after the four flowers that appear most frequently – tulips, carnations, hyacinths and roses – but it is by no means restricted to these alone. This semi-naturalistic plant ornament reflects the style of contemporary court miniature painting, with highly formalized flowers and leafy shrubs arranged in symmetrical groups. The tulips depicted on these tiles have sharply pointed petals; this was no formal exaggeration by the artist – a Turkish treatise specified that the perfect tulip should be shaped like an almond with dagger-like petals.

The appearance of the *quatre fleurs* style coincided with the discovery of a true red. This no doubt encouraged a wider currency for this style since its naturalism was enhanced by using red, rather than blue or green, for the flower-heads, as was its legibility and visual impact.

Chinese elements infiltrated the *quatre fleurs* style too, in the form of the *prunus* blossom. Panels in the Topkapi Saray and the Rustem Pasha mosque feature *prunus* trees against a dark-blue ground; they appear again in the baths at the mosque of Eyub Ensari in a sophisticated design – the *prunus* stems are broken and bent at a sharp angle to fit the confines of the space allowed them and then laced through holes in broad feathery *saz* leaves that mark strong horizontals across the design *(plate 3)*.

There is some dispute as to how far the Iznik designs were directly influenced by the court designers *(nakkāş)* and certainly extant evidence of their involvement is limited. A blue and white *hatayî*-style panel of exceptional quality and complexity, now in the Sunnet Odasi (circumcision kiosk) of the Topkapi Saray was obviously made from pounced cartoons, as were some of the calligraphic panels at Rustem Pasha; but on other tiles the application appears rather mechanical, often stencilled *(plates 5 and 28)* or appearing to be so, judging from the accuracy of the repeats and the lack of freehand brush-strokes.

However, since production at Iznik was so closely linked to imperial architectural schemes it seems likely that general specifications, if not precise instructions and prepared designs, would have been imposed by the court at Istanbul. We know that designs for textiles were prepared by the imperial designers and sent to Bursa to be woven, and the close parallels between textile design, album drawings, illumination and ceramics suggest that Iznik

patterns also originated with the court studios. A comparison of tiles in the *hatayî* style, with illuminated borders from a later sixteenth century manuscript (Album of Murad III (1574-93), now in the Osterreichische National-bibliothek, Vienna) show similarities in the interpretation of motifs, which are surely too strong to have been accidental.

By 1620 the industry at Iznik had fallen into decline. Of the 300 factories flourishing at the height of production, only nine were left in 1648. The expansion of the Ottoman empire was over, and a once-vigorous civilization was increasingly degenerate.

Though Iznik was the chief centre for the production of tiles there were other substantial ceramic industries in the Ottoman provinces, notably in Damascus, Syria. The Syrian industry pre-dates the Ottoman conquest and tiles were produced there in quantity in the early fifteenth century. A revival was fostered from around 1550 by the Ottoman campaigns and the construction of new buildings in Damascus. Though closely related stylistically to contemporary Iznik tiles, the Syrian product is distinguished both by the character of the designs, and by the range of colours. Tiles dating from the second half of the sixteenth century are painted in shades of cobalt blue, turquoise, manganese purple and a green which varies from olive to a distinctive bright apple-colour. This particular combination appears on vessels from Iznik but never on tiles. Rather more crudely executed than those from Iznik, the Syrian tiles are more strongly naturalistic and characterized by a fluid freehand quality. The commonest designs feature vigorous leafy flowering plants, presented as if growing from roots at the base of the tile.

Again the ceramic artists borrowed motifs from other media and other cultures. One tile illustrated here *(plate 32b)* carries a border pattern which is a variation of the *chintamani* motif found on many Ottoman woven textiles. This motif – groups of three circles alternating with double wavy lines – has a complex symbolism originating in Buddhist China where it represented pearls on the waves of the sea and was a symbol of good fortune. Absorbed into Islamic art it was transformed by placing a smaller circle off-centre inside the larger one thus suggesting a crescent shape. This symbol was used by the Turks on their war flag and also as a decorative feature. In the hands of the Syrian artist the wave motifs, no longer horizontal, have lost their original function and become arbitrary decorative elements, and the crescent shape too is distorted by the addition of white dots in the black disc.

A minor tile industry also existed at Diyarbakir in eastern Anatolia. They produced underglaze tiles, similar to those from Iznik though technically inferior. They favoured floral motifs of the simplest kind, but lack of skill resulted in rather cramped and overcrowded designs *(plate 16)*, as in the flower vase framed by an ogival cartouche. This tile also shows the brownish equivalent of Iznik red, produced at Diyarbakir.

BIBLIOGRAPHY

Denny, W, *The Ceramics of the Mosque of Rustem Pasha and the Environment of Change*, New York, 1977.

Lane, A, *A Guide to the Collection of Tiles*, Victoria & Albert Museum, London, 1960.

Lane, A, 'The Ottoman Pottery of Isnik', *Ars Orientalis*, II, 1957.

ed. Petsopoulos, Y, *Tulips, Arabesques and Turbans: Decorative Arts from the Ottoman Empire*, London, 1982.

Rawson, J, *Chinese ornament*, London, British Museum, 1984.

Rogers, J M, *Islamic Art and Design 1500-1700*, London, British Museum, 1983.

KEY TO PLATES

The majority of the plates show Iznik tiles dating from the second half of the sixteenth century. The exceptions are plates 7, 15 and 16 from Diyarbakir, and plates 29, 30, 31a, 31b, 32a and 32b from Damascus, all dated to the sixteenth century.

THE PLATES

3

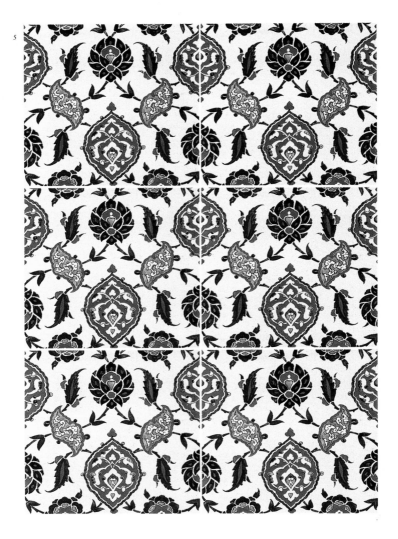

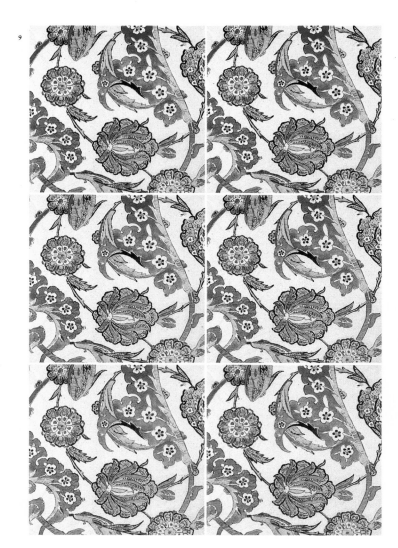

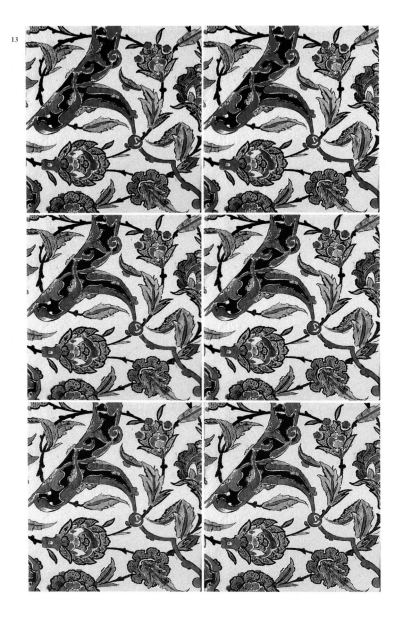

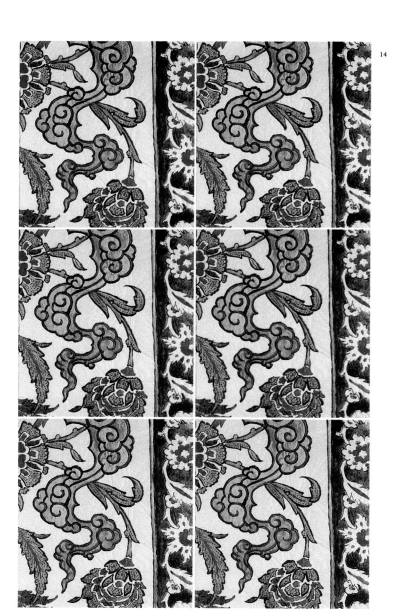

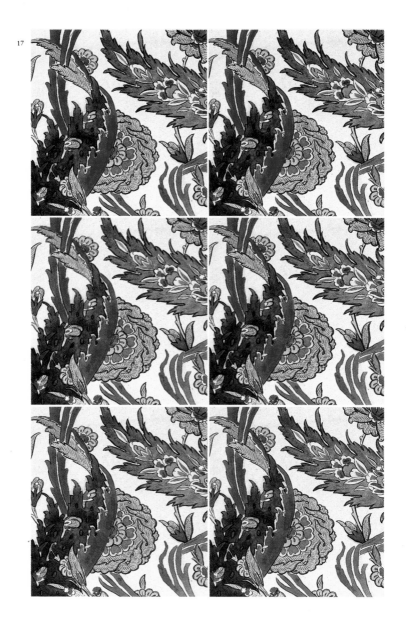

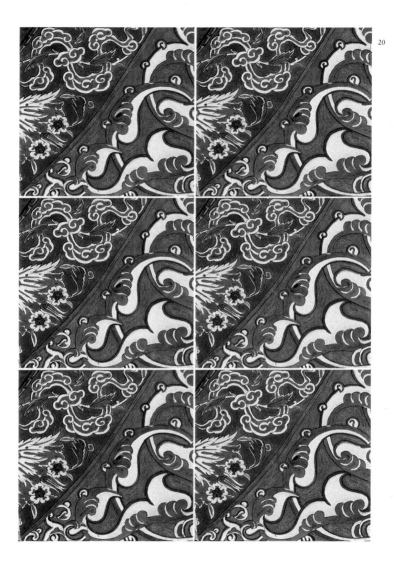

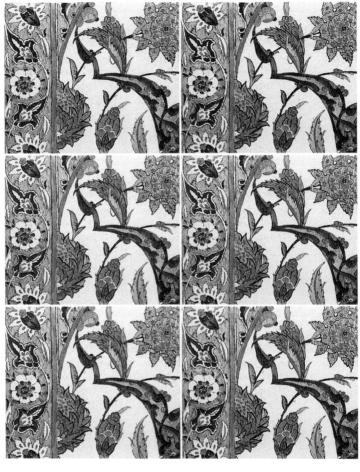

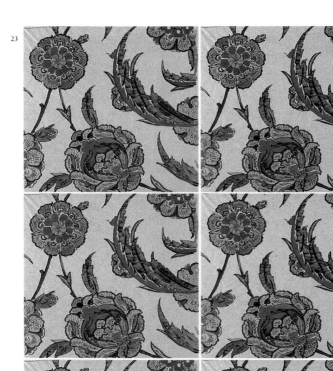

23

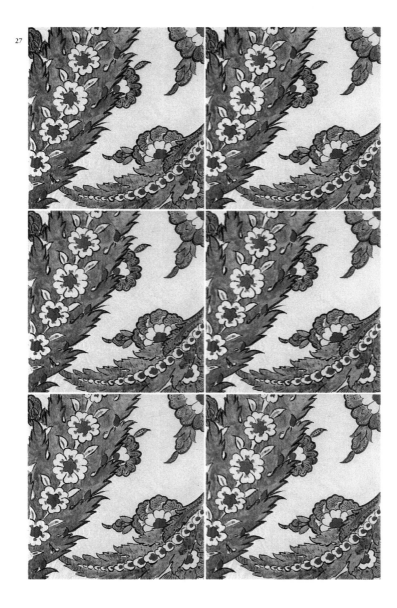

31

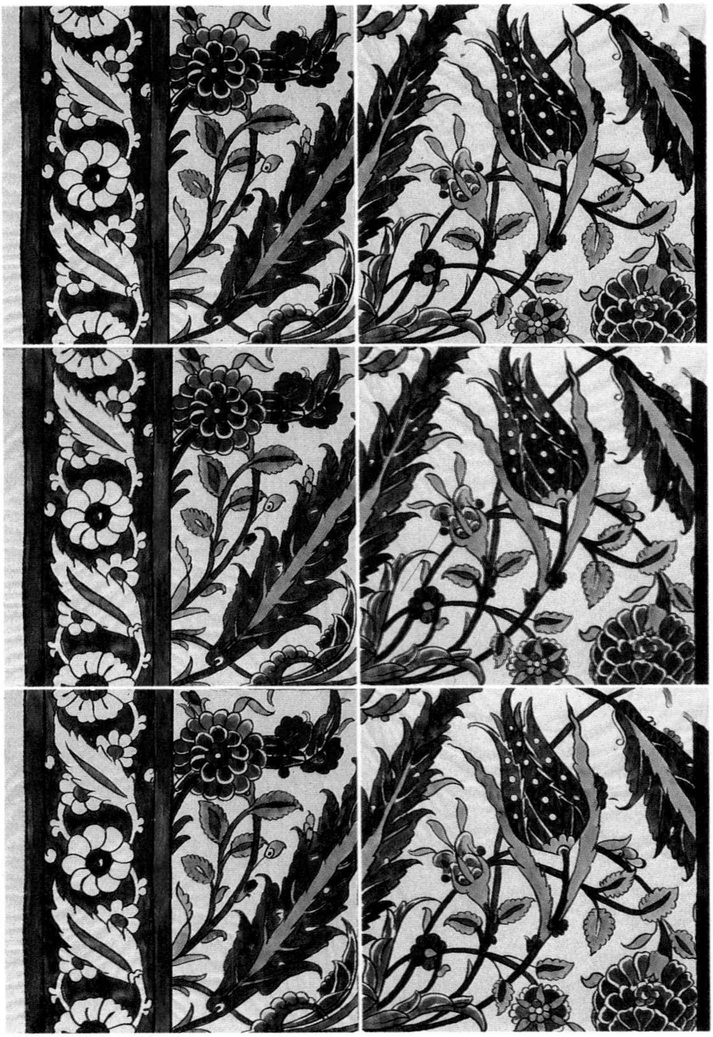